"As a Baptis[...] now w[...] argume[...] [Ji]m addresses in this book. For Christians who are serious about the Bible, serious about morality, and serious about loving their neighbor, addressing long held biases and beliefs about LGBTQ+ people is an imperative place to start. And thanks to this concise, clear and engaging read by Rev. Dr. Jim Dant, you can! The future of the Church will always rest in its ability to respond to God like Peter in Acts 10. As God made whole what had long been understood as profane, Peter was first incredulous, then, curious, and finally and most importantly, converted. Dant's pastoral and prophetic analysis invites us all to our own joyful conversion toward affirmation and inclusion."

Revs. Maria Swearingen and Sally Sarratt,
Senior Co-Pastors, Calvary Baptist Church,
Washington, D.C.

"For those of us who encounter well-meaning family and community members seeking to correct the error of our welcome of the LGBTQ community into the full life and ministry of the church, a brief and Biblically grounded response is found here. I needed this in the '80s when I was a young pastor, and I need it now as the debate over who's 'in' continues to divide people of faith. Could you print mine in a pocket version please?"

Paula Dempsey,
Director of Partnership Relations,
Alliance of Baptists

"Jim Dant offers a gift to LGBTQ people and their friends, families, and fellow congregants who need easily-accessible tools to 'guard their souls' against one-liner putdowns and bumper-sticker degradation. This is truly 'a survival manual for those on the firing line' in which Dant shares many of his own confrontational encounters with Christians who haven't yet gotten the message that LGBTQ people are beloved of God."

The Rev. Cody J. Sanders, PhD,
Pastor of Old Cambridge Baptist Church in
Harvard Square and author of *A Brief Guide to Ministry with LGBTQIA Youth*

This I Know

A Simple Biblical Defense for LGBTQ Christians

JIM DANT

© 2018

Published in the United States by Nurturing Faith Inc.,
Macon GA, www.nurturingfaith.net.

Library of Congress Cataloging-in-Publication Data is
available.

ISBN 978-1-63528-036-4

All rights reserved. Printed in the United States of
America.

Cover photo by Ben Mullinax.

For Dave and Danny
Rest in peace. Live in peace.

ACKNOWLEDGMENTS

My biological father was a veteran of the Vietnam War. I was quite young when he was a soldier, and I have few memories of him. One memory among this limited collection is the night he shared his greatest fear. He was home on leave. The family was gathered around my grandmother's Formica-top dining room table. My five-year-old feet were dangling above the patterned linoleum floor. Completely enamored by his stories of war and guns and napalm and airplanes, I finally asked, "Daddy, are you ever scared?" He paused for a moment, stared thoughtfully out the kitchen window, and said, "Only when we are at the edge of a jungle and the sergeant looks at me and says, 'You go first.' That's when I'm most scared."

I need to thank some people who have dared to go first. Joy Yee, Jennifer Craig, and Judy Snyder were the first to step into this jungle of grammatical errors, misspelled words, and structural puzzlements to help clear and clean a path for others to walk. I'm indebted to their command of the English language, their sensitivity to the reader's eye, their demand for theological consistency, and their respect for my particular style. Thanks for editing.

I am grateful to the membership of First Baptist Church, Greenville, South Carolina. This congregation has consistently been on the frontlines of shaping Baptist faith throughout the decades. They take seriously their commitment to follow Christ. They do not tolerate a shallow reading of the Bible but intentionally struggle with the depth of God's love, the mystery of the Spirit's work, the abundance of Christ's grace, and the inherent fallacies of human insight. It is not always easy to find the truth, and it is much harder to live it. Some have endured the insult and challenge of those who disagree. They step into the jungle bravely.

I am humbled by the faith and courage of the LGBTQ Christians who have allowed me to be their pastor and have trusted First Baptist Greenville to be their spiritual home. It was with trepidation that many stepped into our sanctuary. They wondered if our welcome was a trick and if our love would last. I can't imagine what we have provided these brothers and sisters, but what they have given us is immeasurable.

Finally, thank you for purchasing this book. You are in my prayers. You may be stepping into a jungle.

FOREWORD

The phone call came as a shock. It had to be a practical joke. We were planning a choir tour to the southern United States and were seeking large performing arts venues to rent. The caller said, "The First Baptist Church of Greenville, South Carolina, would like to host the concert." I chuckled. Do you wonder why I thought this was a joke? After all, we're just a choir singing in a church.

I am the artistic director of the San Francisco Gay Men's Chorus. It is the granddaddy of the LGBTQ choral movement that now spans the globe—and one of the largest of its kind. I was bringing 250 singers on tour. We were traveling with the sole purpose of lifting up LGBTQ folks and their allies; we were standing up against discrimination and bigotry. If I know anything from experience, gays and Baptists are two things that do not go together—or so I thought.

Afraid to call Dr. Dant, the church's senior minister, and hear the rejection firsthand, I took the easy way out and emailed him. He responded immediately and said the invitation was indeed genuine. I still did not believe it would actually happen. I have seen far too many church folk in my life offer the hand of friendship only to have their hand (and mine) slapped with Scripture. I did not want to play these kinds of games with my singers' hearts, many of whom have been there all too often. I was skeptical at best and for good reason.

Short version of a long story: In 1986 I was the associate minister of music at First Baptist Church, Houston, and on the faculty of Houston Baptist University. I had a beautiful wife and two children—the "perfect" life—but I was living a lie. I came out. It did not go well; I lost everything.

Now, here I was, 30-plus years later, with a Baptist church welcoming me and mine with no caveats. It was an unconditional welcome and embrace. Amid local criticism—even threats—the church was allowing us to perform.

We had no idea if anyone would attend. At 7:30 on that October Friday night, we entered a sanctuary filled to the rafters, standing room only, chairs brought in for the overflow. As the first singer entered the hall, the congregation stood to its feet and applauded. The applause continued until the last man reached the front of the sanctuary. The chorus wept as they took their places. Never in our wildest dreams did we imagine the wall would come tumbling down before our very eyes. It was a life-changing, healing moment for me and for the singers.

And now there is this beautiful book. I love it so much. I love the seriousness of it and, even more, the humor in it. It is who we are. It explains in very clear messages how we got to this impasse. And it gives us the bricks each of us needs to start building a bridge to one another.

Jim, thank you for writing this amazing book. Thank you for believing. Thank you for having the courage to do what you are doing and for leading the way against overwhelming odds. You are my hero.

Dr. Tim Seelig
Artistic Director
San Francisco Gay Men's Chorus

CONTENTS

INTRODUCTION

Jesus loves me, this I know.
For the Bible tells me so.

The words to "Jesus Loves Me" are among our earliest musical memories of faith and church. For most of us, they are words of assurance and comfort. We rest into them when life is complex. We hold to them when faith feels unmoored. We trust them when we cannot wrap our minds or our prayers around anything else. The simple tune and lyrics remind us we are accepted and our acceptance is confirmed in sacred text.

These same words may ring hollow in the ears of a member of the LGBTQ community. They learned the tune as children. They memorized the words. They delighted in the idea of being

1

cherished by God and guarded by Scripture. But somewhere along the way, someone in the church turned the Bible into a weapon and Jesus into an inaccessible friend. Many of the LGBTQ people I've come to know have had to learn to trust this song again. They've had to be reintroduced to the Jesus who loves them and to the Bible that guards them. I want my LGBTQ brothers and sisters to know Jesus loves them and the Bible says no different.

There is no valid, Christian, biblical argument against same-sex relationships between consenting adults. If you believe this but struggle to explain it to others, read on. If you do not believe this but truly wonder how LGBTQ supportive Christians read the Bible differently than you, read on.

I receive multiple voicemails, emails, and social media messages each week from other Christians—conservative, angry, uncomfortably inquisitive—wanting to know how I can be welcoming and affirming of LGBTQ Christians when the Bible is *clearly* against homosexuality.

They always ask, "Haven't you read the Bible?" I rarely answer or return these calls and messages. There isn't time. But in my mind I have rehearsed the speech a hundred times: "I've been reading the Bible all my life. Really. I've been in love with the Bible my whole life. I'm a Bible geek. I read it at home, in Sunday school, in Vacation Bible School, in youth Bible studies, in college, in seminary, and in decades of sermon preparation. I've taught biblical studies in churches, universities, seminaries, retreats, camps, and conferences."

I'm not into competitively comparing, but I'm certain I've read the Bible more often and more thoroughly than almost all my callers and critics. I wish I could take the time to share with each of them—and I wish they were truly receptive to—what I've found regarding LGBTQ Christians in biblical text. But they cling tightly to the English rendering of an ancient text from a culture that existed 2,000 years ago. Ironically, the Bible is clear on the subject, but clearly not in the way they think. There is no valid, Christian, biblical argument against same-sex relationships between consenting adults. Persons may argue against LGBTQ identities, relationships, and rights based upon economic, political, or personal perspectives. But the Bible cannot credibly be used as a weapon in these fights.

So allow me to say it again—over and over again: There is no valid, Christian, biblical argument against same-sex relationships between consenting adults. However, average LGBTQ Christians (and in fact, the average straight Christian who loves and supports them) do not have the biblical savvy to defend themselves against the barrage of assaults and/or kind, well-meaning sermons spoken against them. These assaults and sermons are characterized by Bible verses lifted from their historical and theological contexts and used to bludgeon the listener. Most books presenting an LGBTQ-favorable interpretation of biblical texts are so complex and theologically deep that the average reader gets lost in the academia. The majority of progressives and liberals tend to

speak in paragraphs rather than sound bites...
long paragraphs...with footnotes. These type
volumes are necessary in legitimizing biblical
interpretations, however, our friends and loved
ones are living in a culture that confronts them
with single lines and single verses. The victims of
these visceral attacks need simple verbiage with
which they can respond or at least guard their
souls.

Hence, this small volume is not intended to
be a thorough theological discussion of sexuality in the biblical text. Rather, it is a survival
manual for those on the firing line. I've laid aside
the paragraphs and adopted the 'bumper sticker/
sound bite methodology' of the opposition. The
first section will provide simple responses to the
typical verses and theologies unfairly imposed upon
LGBTQ persons. The second section will provide
the church with broad theological 'hand holds' for
welcoming and affirming the faith, worth, contri-
butions, and journey of LGBTQ Christians. I've
chosen a simple format in which I will present a

challenge, an appropriate response, and a brief explanation. And just for fun (in order to keep the reading lite and shed some light on the insanity I deal with on a regular basis), I'll share a few stories and thoughts from actual conversations.

If you find these words and arguments overstated and/or oversimplified, good. Mission accomplished. Again, this is not an exhaustive theological explanation. It is a simple biblical defense for those whom Jesus loves.

PART I

The LGBTQ Christian and the Bible

1. Leviticus Says It's an Abomination

The Challenge
The Bible says in Leviticus 18:22, "You shall not lie with a man as with a woman; it is an abomination."

The Response (#1)
I am a Christian, and I have been freed from the demands of Old Testament law. And if you are a Christian, I assume you do not live by Old Testament law either.

The Explanation (#1)
No Christian who challenges you with a verse from Leviticus is living according to the laws of Leviticus. I guarantee it. Many judgmental Christians find it convenient to impose the laws of Leviticus on others while claiming graceful exclusion for themselves. And do not let them convince you that some laws are 'moral' and others may be disregarded as 'less important.' According to Leviticus it is also an abomination to eat shrimp, wear clothing of mixed fabric, and touch the sick or the dead. According to Leviticus we are supposed to stone—

in other words, put to death—persons who do not keep Sabbath, who talk back to their parents, or who commit adultery. No one who claims to be a follower of Jesus accepts these as normative standards or necessary demands.

Just for Fun

I was leading a conference at Scarritt Bennett Center of Vanderbilt University several years ago. The title of my session was "Loving Leviticus: What Every Christian Should Know about the Heart of the Torah." I had made my way through much of the book without mentioning homosexuality (which, comparatively, is a minor part of levitical law). Finally, a frustrated young zealot raised his hand. I acknowledged him.

"When are you going to mention the sin of homosexuality?" he asked.

"Do you believe it's a sin?" I responded.

Enthusiastically, he asserted, "Yes, it is!"

I calmly asked him, "Are you homosexual?"

"No! Absolutely not!"

I continued, "Do you eat cheeseburgers?"

9

"Heck yeah! I love cheeseburgers."

"Well, then, you are a homosexual."

He was beside himself. "I am not! What's a cheeseburger got to do with it?"

I responded, "The New Testament book of James says, 'Whoever keeps the whole law but fails in one point has become accountable for all of it.' It's against the laws of Leviticus to eat beef and milk together. You've broken that law. If you break one law, you're guilty of all laws. Therefore, since you eat cheeseburgers, you are a homosexual."

No Christian who challenges you with a verse from Leviticus is living according to the laws of Leviticus. And according to the New Testament, even if they tried, they would still be guilty of every law in the text when they break just one.

***

The Challenge

The Bible says in Leviticus 18:22, "You shall not lie with a man as with a woman; it is an abomination."

The Response (#2)

This verse refers to treating another person like property. I do not treat my partner like property; I treat my partner with love and respect.

The Explanation (#2)

We've already approached this verse from a contextual perspective—it is one verse in a corpus of law we do not, cannot, and need not embrace. But it's important to note that the verse itself does not forbid a consensual, healthy relationship between persons of the same sex. It does forbid treating another person like property. This is the real issue of Leviticus 18:22.

According to other verses in Leviticus 18, we are also commanded to avoid "the nakedness of" (engaging in sexual relations with) our aunts, sisters-in-law, nieces, and other females. However, if the spouses of these females died, the male elder was obligated to marry, sleep with, and produce children with these women. Sleeping with them prior to their spouses' deaths was not a moral issue, but a property issue. I do not delight in this cultural reality, but women were primarily considered property during the writing of these laws.

So when the law says, "You shall not lie with a man as with a woman," it is a prohibition from treating another man like property. Women could be told or forced to sleep with their male caregivers. They had little or no choice in this matter. But a man could not treat another man this way. A man could not treat another man like property. This has nothing, however, to do with consensual relationships between men.

Just for Fun

I have at times found it necessary to illuminate individuals with regard to the perilous extent of their reliance on Leviticus as a weapon against LGBTQ Christians.

The office phone rang on a Wednesday afternoon. I lifted the receiver and heard our receptionist speak a familiar line: "I'm sending a call through to you. I think it's another holy anger call." I chuckled and said, "Put him through."

I had barely said hello and offered my name before the sermon began. He loudly shared with me—in his words—the authorized King James Version of several verses, ending with a confident recitation of Leviticus 18:22. I finally slipped into a slight break in his speech and said, "I'm not sure any of us truly wants to live according to the laws of Leviticus."

Surprisingly, he responded, "I'm willing to live by every single law in the book if it will rid the world of homosexuals."

I calmly challenged him, "You realize that if we embrace the standards of Leviticus with regard to sexuality, we will find ourselves legitimizing sex trafficking, slavery, and a host of other crimes against women. Old Testament law allows for the sale and trade of daughters. I hope we are past treating anyone like property—not just males."

He hung up.

***

2. Creation—Adam and Eve, Not Adam and Steve

The Challenge
The creation story of Genesis 2 explicitly and exclusively defines marriage as the union of one man and one woman.

The Response
The creation story of Genesis refers to humanity's need for companionship and God's care for that need. It was never intended to establish heterosexual parameters for marriage.

The Explanation
Outside the laws of Leviticus, no biblical text has been referenced more than Genesis 2 in attempts to discount the LGBTQ Christian. The ever familiar, "God created Adam and Eve, not Adam and Steve" has become a mantra for many anti-gay protestors. For many scholars, the easiest refute of this mindset would simply be to remind readers that the first eleven chapters of Genesis are poetic, mythical stories recorded to give the God

of Israel credit for creation and the expansion of humankind. The writers and early readers of these stories would have never taken them literally as many do today. However, for argument's sake, I am willing to read and interpret the text from the more literal perspective of my protesting brothers and sisters. From this perspective I must note, their interpretation of this story lessens the breadth and beauty of God's care for humanity.

A close reading of the story reveals God's true impetus for the creation of a second human. God noticed and decided to remedy the man's loneliness. God's first creative inclination, however, was not a woman…but animals! These animals were paraded before the man, each was named, but none could completely cure the loneliness. With the creation of woman, the man finally exclaims, "This is at last bone of bone and flesh of my flesh…" If we interpret the story as a basis for marriage, we have to ask, did God really think the man would marry one of the animals? Were these viable options for marriage? Surely God wasn't toying with the man's emotions! No. God was not marriage matchmaking in this text. God was presenting real options for companionship and community. In fact, many today find meaningful companionship from their pets. People often speak of their pets (and to their pets) in near-human terms and tones. Pets are referred to as children, grand-dogs, man's best friend and on and on and on. God's intent was to provide the man with companionship and a sense of community in his loneliness.

Complete community, however, could only be found in a creature that was "bone of my bone and flesh of my flesh" and at the same time different. Companionship is enjoyed with one who is relatable but unique. I'm not interested in spending time with a clone of myself. I want someone who understands me, but at the same time, embodies a unique sense of self and holds differing ideas. The fact that the man claims the woman as his wife is secondary to the initial intent of this story. God's intent was companionship and community.

The additional posited idea that procreation with same-sex relationships is not possible and thus is contrary to Genesis 1 is a weak argument.

Many heterosexual couples are unable to procreate yet this makes their companionship and marriage no less valid. Many heterosexual couples choose to be childless and this does not invalidate their companionship and marriage. Sexuality within these marriages is exclusively for the purpose of pleasure and intimacy; the celebration of companionship.

By the time we reach Genesis 4, a child of Adam and Eve is venturing into the world. He both fears others that inhabit the world and eventually marries another that inhabits the world. God has been creating people—different people...different kinds of people—throughout the world. It would be near-sighted to believe (particularly since they were feared) the other populations of the world were exactly like those created in Genesis 1 and 2. We live in a diverse world. God infused this world with diversity. We seem to appreciate it in every facet of creation—animals, flower, foliage, landscapes—but can't quite affirm it in each other.

The creation stories of Genesis were not written to promote heterosexual exclusivity in marriage, but rather to convey the wonder and diversity of God's creation. This diversity easily and sacredly includes the creation of LGBTQ individuals and the companionship, marriages, and community they enjoy. Any interpretation of these stories that presses humanity into a single mold lessens the breadth and beauty of God's creation.

Just for Fun

The advertisement was posted on a student bulletin board at Georgia State University—A Bible Study for People Who Have Never Read the Bible. I was intrigued. I was a youth minister at the time. I read the Bible every day. I had read the Bible my whole life. But I wondered who would show up and what the leader would say.

We met on a Tuesday morning in a side room of the campus library. I was one of five who attended. The others were all international students. I put on my best ignorant, albeit, Caucasian face. The leader – a young, zealous university student - began reading from The Gospel of John, Chapter 1, "In the beginning was the Word, and the Word was with God, and the Word was God. 2He was in the beginning with God. 3All things came into being through him, and without him not one thing came into being." Being a tad more conservative than me, he took the group back to Genesis 1 and explained that God, Jesus and the Holy Spirit were present together at creation. He used this idea to explain God's verbiage in Genesis 1, "Let us make man in our image."

"The trinity," he explained, "was what God meant when he used the word 'us.'"

At this point, a young Egyptian student raised his hand.

"You believe God, Jesus and the Holy Spirit created the world?"

"Yes," our leader excitedly responded, "Exactly!"

"Do you believe God is male?"

"Well," replied our leader, "the Bible uses the words 'he' and 'father' when it speaks of God, so I typically refer to God in masculine terms."

"And Jesus was a man?" the Egyptian student further questioned.

"Of course," said our teacher. "He was a real man, born two thousand years ago, to a woman named Mary."

"And is this Holy Spirit a man?" my fellow student asked.

A little less certain in his speech, our near fearless leader responded, "It's hard to say that a spirit is male or female, but since Jesus and God are referred to as male, I think it's appropriate to assume their spirit is male."

A long pause gave room for the Egyptian student to process the information. Finally, he broke the silence.

"I have read creation stories from other cultures and religions. All of them have a male and female God who through sexual intercourse brought forth the earth. But in the Christian faith, it is just three men that birthed the world. This is strange. Other faiths believe the world was created through a typical heterosexual process, but your faith only has three men. Does this mean that the highest form of relationship and creativity exists in a same-sex relationship?"

Quickly and anxiously our leader responded, "Those are pagan notions of creation. Our creation story has nothing to do with sexuality."

It has always amazed me how others read our stories of faith when they have not been forced to wear the doctrinal lenses we wear. And how ironic that we deplete our creation stories of gender and sexuality until we need these caveats to control or persecute another.

***

3. Deuteronomy Says Transgender People Are Abhorrent

The Challenge
Deuteronomy 22:5 states that it is abhorrent to God for a man to wear women's clothing or a woman to wear men's clothing. Therefore, it is a sin to live a transgender life.

The Response
I am a Christian and I have been freed from the demands of Old Testament law. In addition, the ideas of 'abhorrence and abomination' were a reference to ceremonial cleanliness and were not moral labels.

The Explanation
As mentioned in *The Response*, the terms *abhorrence* and *abomination* have been completely misunderstood and poorly communicated in contemporary language. In our modern vernacular, these words carry a moral connotation that was not part of their original meaning or intent. The primary purpose of Old Testament laws was to make or keep a

person (primarily a man) ritually clean so that he might enter the temple for worship. Anything that made the person unclean was labeled an abomination. Being sick, touching a dead person, not washing one's hands according to specified ritual, wearing mixed-fiber clothing—all of these made one ritually unclean to enter the temple but were never considered moral issues.

With this understanding of abomination in mind, a man would never wear a woman's clothing or allow a woman to wear his clothing because she was likely 'ritually unclean.' Women, by nature of biology and role, were typically unclean. Their menstrual cycles made them unclean, and the process of purification from a menstrual cycle kept them unclean for most of the month. Touching any bodily discharge made a person unclean; women tended to the runny noses and soiled garments of children. Touching the sick or the dead made one unclean; women traditionally cared for the sick and prepared the dead for burial. Because of their constant uncleanness, women were not even allowed to touch the clothing of a man and vice versa. This was the issue in the New Testament story of the bleeding woman who touched the hem of Jesus' robe. She was breaking the law. She would have transferred her ritually impurity to Jesus by touching his clothing.

Just for Fun

The command of Deuteronomy 22:5 has nothing to do with style of clothing or what we refer to today as 'cross dressing.' Everyone in the biblical era 'cross dressed.' The garments of men and women were primarily the same style; everyone wore dresses in the Middle East! Tunics, wraps, cloaks, sashes, and scarves were the functional attire of both men and women. It would have been impossible to know if a cloak was feminine or masculine. Again, the issue was an unclean person touching your garments if you wanted to remain ritually clean for temple admittance.

While we have gender-differentiated much of our clothing today, many functional items do not differ at all. My three daughters have stolen most of my sweatshirts, sweaters, and jackets. (If any of them are reading this, I'd like them returned, please.)

***

4. Sodom and Gomorrah

The Challenge
God destroyed the people of Sodom and Gomorrah because of their homosexual behavior.

The Response
The Bible says God destroyed Sodom and Gomorrah because of their failure to practice hospitality and their lack of care for the needy in their community.

The Explanation
The story of Sodom and Gomorrah is recorded in Genesis 18–19. To read this story as an indictment against homosexuality is to *completely*—and I mean *completely*—miss the point of the story. Hospitality is a central tenet of Jewish culture and Jewish law. The primary sin of Sodom and Gomorrah was their lack of hospitality toward the stranger.

In this story, two strangers come to Sodom and Gomorrah. Lot, a kinsman of Abraham, takes the strangers into his home (hospitality). The men of the city come to Lot's door and ask that the strangers be sent outside so they can 'know them.' The context of the story is clear: they want to have sex with the strangers. Lot, however, chooses to guard them in his home (hospitality). He lives well the role of host. He does not necessarily hold the moral high ground when it comes to sexuality, however. In fact, he is so intent on practicing acceptable hospitality to the strangers that he offers his daughters to the men at his door: "Look, I have two daughters who have not known a man; let me bring them out to you, and do to them as you please; only do nothing to these men, for they have come under the shelter of my roof" (hospitality). Remember, women were property and could be traded, sold, or given away for the purpose of rape.

When Sodom and Gomorrah are destroyed, Lot and his family are saved for their righteous act. Righteous act? Would the typical critic of homosexuality be willing to affirm the righteousness of a man who offers his daughters up for a gang rape? No. The issue in this story has nothing to do with sexuality and/or the morality surrounding it. These cities were not destroyed for being gay. If sexual morality and practice were the issues, surely gang rape was not better than homosexuality in the eyes of God. Lot's 'righteous act' was his practice of hospitality. He cared for the stranger, the outcast, and the needy at all cost.

In fact, the only biblical reference that specifically cites and explains why Sodom and Gomorrah were destroyed appears in Ezekiel 16:49: "This was the guilt of your sister Sodom: she and her daughters had pride, excess of food, and prosperous ease, but did not aid the poor and needy. They were haughty, and did abominable things before me; therefore I removed them when I saw it." As we've already stated, Leviticus lists a multitude of abominations. But the primary reasons stated by Ezekiel have nothing to do with sexuality and everything to do with hospitality and the care of the community.

Just for Fun

I was invited to teach a Sunday school class in the Atlanta area almost two decades ago. They asked me to speak about the 'Sin of Sodom.' The gathered young adults were trying to—in their words—gain ammunition against the growing influence and agenda of the gay community. I shared the following words.

In my judgment, there is a great irony in the use of Sodom and Gomorrah as an indictment against homosexuals. The story actually suggests God destroyed a people because they were not hospitable to those from outside their community. The citizens of Sodom and Gomorrah were more intent on stripping these strangers of their identity and dignity than welcoming them into the community. Lot, the one who welcomed and protected, was saved. But he was not saved because of sexual morality. His saving grace was his hospitality. Those who were inhospitable and uncaring were the ones destroyed.

Those who strip LGBTQ Christians of their God-given identity, their dignity, and their place in the faith community are the ones committing the sin of Sodom and Gomorrah. Churches, parents, and 'Christian schools' are rejecting gay and transgendered sons, daughters, students, church members, and friends, often leaving them homeless and alone. This is not practicing hospitality. This is not providing sanctuary for the stranger and the outsider. The peril these self-righteous people of faith pronounce on others may be the very peril of which they are in danger. How ironic.

***

5. Jesus Defined Marriage as One Woman and One Man

The Challenge

Jesus defines marriage as a relationship between a man and a woman, not between persons of the same sex. That's why Jesus said, "Have you not read that the one who made them at the beginning 'made them male and female'?... For this reason a man shall leave his father and mother and be joined to his wife, and the two shall become one flesh. So they are no longer two, but one flesh. Therefore what God has joined together, let no one separate" (Matt 19:4–6).

The Response

Jesus is not defining marriage in this statement. Jesus is answering a specific question posed in verse 3, regarding divorce: "Is it lawful for a man to divorce his wife for any cause?" (Matt 19:3). The question references a man and a wife. Jesus' use of the terms man and wife is simply reflective of the question asked.

The Explanation

These verses are oft promoted as Jesus' definition of marriage. This is a gross overstatement—filled with assumption—regarding Jesus' thoughts. Jesus was simply answering a question about the divorce of a man and woman. That's all. The obvious subject and object of the sentence are 'a man and a wife.' Jesus' words are specific to the question asked. Jesus was not asked about a man and a man, nor was he asked about a woman and a woman. He answered the question asked, and nothing else can be surmised regarding these words.

If I were asked, "Is it okay to leave carrots out of vegetable soup?" and I responded negatively or affirmatively, I would only be answering the 'soup question' at hand. It could not be further assumed that I only eat vegetable soup, or I do not support the eating of chicken noodle soup or that soup is the only valid meal for humans. I'm only answering the question at hand, not creating universal soup parameters.

Just for Fun

I always chuckle when I hear someone make reference to 'biblical family values' or 'Bible-based marriage.' They are usually referring to biblical phrases lifted out of context or ideologies they assume are in the Bible but, alas, are only part of their cultural dogma. Most modern Christians speaking of biblical family values are actually pressing their cultural norms and beliefs on the text. The norms and beliefs do not arise from an honest and thorough reading of the text.

I mean, really, have you ever thought about the family models presented in the Bible? Abraham married Sarah, his half-sister—the daughter of Abraham's father, but not his mother. Isaac's family sent a servant to "find a wife for Isaac." Jacob married sisters Leah and Rachel. He not only had children with both sisters, but also—with his wives' permission—with his wives' servants.

According to Deuteronomy 22, if a woman is raped and the rapist is caught, the perpetrator must pay the young woman's father fifty shekels of silver and marry the young woman. (Are we uncomfortable yet?)

David had multiple wives and several concubines. His son, Solomon, had 700 wives and 300 concubines. I think you get the picture. An honest perusal of biblical family systems makes it obvious that they look nothing like marriage and family today. Some will argue that these examples simply fall short of the 'ideal.' If that is the case, *every* biblical family system—every one—falls short of the ideal. And yet, these were cherished children of God—part of God's family and God's work in the world. None of their family situations disqualified them from relationship and relevance in God's kingdom.

The fact is, like it or not, marriage is a culturally defined institution. This covenant expression between individuals differs from culture to culture and has shifted within particular cultures through time. There is nothing wrong with cultures establishing traditions, ethics, and morals. Many would say it is necessary for lawful and healthy society. This is why I stated in the introduction that positions on homosexuality may be argued from economic, political, or personal opinion. But the Bible should not be used as a weapon in this fight. The ideas of marriage, relationships, and sexuality are dynamic and a tad messy in Holy Scripture.

***

6. Paul Says Homosexuality Is a Sin

The Challenge

Even if you do not follow the Old Testament law and even if Jesus did not intentionally define marriage, the apostle Paul is absolutely clear in his writings: homosexuality is a sin. Just read Romans 1:26–27, 1 Corinthians 6:9, and 1 Timothy 1:10.

The Response

Paul is writing about rape, pedophilia, and temple prostitution—all nonconsensual sexual relations between a lesser and a greater power. I'm against those things too. Paul is not writing about consensual, healthy relationships between adults.

The Explanation

In Paul's letters to the church at Corinth and to his young protégé Timothy, he uses the Greek word *arsenokotoi* to refer to a specific sin. The first time the word was translated *homosexuality* in an English Bible was in 1946. The word appears very few times in the Bible, and nowhere in biblical literature is it self-defined or explained. Our only hints to its true meaning lie outside the Bible. In non-biblical Greek literature, the word is typically used to reference two acts: 1) sexuality between gods and humans and 2) the sexual use of women in temple prostitution. In both cases, a more powerful entity acts upon a weaker entity. The sin implied by this strange word is best understood as any sexual act forced upon another—namely, rape or pedophilia.

In Greek mythology, the gods often had their way with humans. Wealthy and powerful Greek citizens obtained servants—often minors—for the purpose of sexual gratification. The possession of these 'servants' was a symbol of power and a vain reflection of the gods' use of humans.

There is absolutely no reason to assume this word refers to healthy relationships between same-sex, consenting adults. In fact, the word appears over 70 times in Greek manuscripts outside the New Testament, and in those manuscripts it *never*—not once—refers to homosexuality.

It is in Paul's letter to the Romans that he mentions natural versus unnatural acts between same-sex individuals. The minds of many readers go immediately to consensual homosexuality, but this is not the case. Again, it is important to understand what was considered 'natural' in the first century. It was not considered 'natural' for a man to treat another man like property. The tone of this text is aggressive in nature. Lust, degradation, and consumption are the impetus behind the listed acts. In fact, verse 27 implies this consumptive, negative passion was just as prevalent among heterosexuals and should be avoided in that population as well. Paul is in no way referencing a loving, healthy, relationship between consenting same-sex couples.

Likewise, we must remember the 'natural' role of women in the first century. It cannot be overlooked that Romans 1:26 refers to the females as "their women." Women were still primarily considered property. They were property and it was expected for them to be cared for by a responsible *male* party. They were expected to be passive in life and especially sexuality. For a woman to take an active role in sexuality would be unnatural. It would also be unnatural for a woman to care for or please the property of another. Again, Paul is not referring to the moral problem of homosexuality, but rather the crumbling of what was considered 'natural' societal norms with regard to property and the role of that property.

I would also argue that the life God has given us is diminished and unappreciated if we try to be something we inherently are not. It would be unnatural for LGBTQ persons to try to be something other than what God created them to be. This, in fact, was a part of what the church has called 'original sin.' Adam and Eve attempted to be something they were not—eat the fruit and you will be like God. The result was their shame of their nakedness. God asked them, "Who told you you were naked?" In other words, who told you the way I created you was something of which to be ashamed? Why are you ashamed of who/what I created you to be?

If a person carries shame and/or guilt over their sexual orientation or gender identity, someone other than God placed it on them.

Just for Fun

Almost three decades ago I received a call from a county school board representative in a southern state. She requested that I participate in a 'sex education forum' sponsored by the school board. Several board representatives were concerned about the current curriculum and its openness to contraception and homosexuality. I asked why I had been chosen as a participant. She quickly and confidently responded, "Because you are a Baptist preacher! You know the Bible. We know you will speak against the encouragement of condom distribution and, more importantly, any leniency toward homosexuality in the curriculum." I assured her she did not want me to participate in the forum. Adamantly, she begged me to reconsider: "We need a strong Christian voice." I responded, "My strong Christian voice will have to assert that there is no valid Christian, biblical argument against same-sex relationships between consenting adults. You may choose to argue against homosexuality on the basis of politics, economics, or personal opinion, but there is no credible Christian, biblical argument against a consensual relationship between two adults."

She hung up.

***

7. Practicing Homosexuals Have Not Repented

The Challenge

You cannot be Christian if you are a practicing homosexual because you have not repented of your sin.

The Response

One, I do not believe that 'being who God created me to be' is a sin. And two, even if it was a sin, my present relationship with God and my future with God are a product of my faith in the grace of God. My relationship with God is not dependent upon my works.

The Explanation

This is the most astoundingly illogical statement made by Christians with regard to persons in the LGBTQ community. I've heard it numerous times, and I'm still shaking my head. The idea that an LGBTQ person cannot claim to be Christian because they still live as an LGBTQ person, engage in LGBTQ sexual activities, or do not fully suppress their attraction to persons of the same sex is flawed theology.

First, the idea that anything must be done— some work or act—in order to earn a relationship with God is completely contrary to the New Testament. Protestant Christianity overwhelmingly affirms this. Almost every Christian preacher proclaims this. We are saved by grace through faith, not works! The early church wrestled with this numerous times and finally settled the issue. Just read the book of Acts or the letters of Paul. Do gentiles have to be circumcised to have a relationship with God? No! Does an Ethiopian eunuch have to denounce his Ethiopian citizenship or reverse his castration to have a relationship with God? No! Did the thief on the cross hanging next to Jesus have to be baptized to spend eternity in paradise with Jesus? No!

The New Testament—and Paul in particular—argues over and over again that no action on our part makes us Christian. It is the gift of God based on our desire to be in relationship with God. And once we recognize that we are God's children,

God is with us wherever we go. The evangelical Christian community has consistently preached salvation by grace alone, but they seem to have found an exception for the LGBTQ community. The LGBTQ community has a host of hoops to hop through before some churches—some Christians—will accept them and their faith.

The primary argument against LGBTQ Christians is that they haven't repented; they still engage in activities deemed sinful. Therefore, they must not have genuinely repented and can't be Christian. (Okay…I'm taking a deep breath. I'm trying to calm down.)

Okay. Let's assume that all LGBTQ persons are walking blobs of sin. Everything they think, say, and do is sinful. And these walking blobs of sin truly want a relationship with God. They sincerely pray for God's grace, are baptized, and unite their life with the church, but they continue to live according to the drives and desires of their life. They may even try their best to avoid some behaviors or relationships and attempt to nurture other behaviors considered more 'normative.' But, alas, they spend their life living as an LGBTQ person. Well, according to their accusers, they are not Christian because they never really repented. Interesting…

Have any of us completely rid our lives of all sinful behavior? No. Not one of us is perfect. And most of us are still struggling with the same crap we were struggling with years ago. By the criteria of the critics, not even the apostle Paul could claim to be a Christian. Remember what he wrote in his letter to the Romans…the last of his letters…the one he wrote years into his faith? "I do not do the good I want, but the evil I do not want is what I do" (Rom 7:19).

Repentance is simply changing the direction and focus of our lives. It is the graceful shift from moving away from God to moving toward God. It is not a demand for perfection.

Just for Fun
I rarely answer the telephone in my office. I intentionally allow all calls to go to voicemail so I can screen them. This is not because I'm private

or uninterested in the lives of my parishioners. However, after our church began to welcome and include the LGBTQ community into our family of faith, I received hundreds—yes, hundreds—of angry phone calls, emails, and messages. So I now let all calls go to voicemail. Every once in a while, though, reflex takes over. The phone rings and like Pavlov's dog, I reach, lift, and then think, "Uh oh."

On one such 'uh oh call,' I had the privilege of speaking with a fellow minister from a Midwestern state. He informed me that I was a false teacher and that I was not following 'God's written word' by allowing gays to participate in the life of the church.

I asked, "Exactly which parts of God's Word am I not following?'

Having a real sense of savvy he said, "Well, I know you're going to say we don't have to follow the Old Testament law. So I'm talking about the words of the New Testament: 'Repent and be baptized for the forgiveness of your sins.' Those gays may be baptized, but if they are still in a relationship with another gay, they haven't repented."

"So let me make sure I understand. If they are still in a relationship that you feel is outside the will of God, you believe they have not repented and therefore cannot be Christian."

"That's what the word of God says, brother," he proudly responded.

I paused. Then I asked him, "Are you married?"

"Yes, I am. To a woman!" he proudly retorted.

"Was she the first woman you had ever slept with?"

"I'm not sure that's any of your business," he tentatively mumbled, "but no. I was a little wilder when I was younger, but I've repented of those sins."

"Interesting," I mused aloud. "Did you know that in 1 Corinthians 6:16—in the New Testament—Paul says that if you sleep with a woman, the 'two of you become one flesh'? Paul believed that sleeping with someone was the moment in which marriage occurred. Nowhere in the New Testament does it say marriage is the result of a vow and a piece of paper. Paul says when you sleep together, you are made one flesh. God joins you together. And what God joins together, no one should separate. Do you realize that you are living in adultery? The woman you are living with is not your real wife. And unless you find and marry the first person you slept with, you have not truly repented. Because you believe that if you are still in a relationship outside the will of God, you have not repented and you cannot be a Christian."

He hung up.

***

8. The Bible Does Not Affirm Homosexual Relationships

The Challenge
There are no homosexual relationships affirmed in the Bible, so it's obvious God's people are not intended to live this way.

The Response
The Bible is typically not concerned with a person's sexual orientation or gender identity. But the Bible may suggest that characters such as Ruth and Naomi, as well as David and Jonathan, participated in same-sex relationships.

The Explanation
We read stories and lines through the lens with which we are most comfortable. We tend to interpret words and phrases to suit our sensitivities.

In the Old Testament book of Ruth, Naomi's husband, Elimelek, and her two sons die. Naomi is left with no male caregiver in her life. She has been living in Moab and decides to return to her hometown of Bethlehem. Her daughters-in-law accompany her on the way until Naomi demands they turn back. One daughter-in-law, Orpah, returns to Moab. Ruth, however, makes the following request of Naomi: "Do not press me to leave you or to turn back from following you! Where you go, I will go; where you lodge, I will lodge; your people shall be my people, and your God my God. Where you die, I will die—there will I be buried. May the Lord do thus and so to me, and more as well, if even death parts me from you!" (Ruth 1:16-17).

Some scholars feel it reasonable to assume Ruth was inviting Naomi into a mutual, caring relationship. Those who disagree might quickly argue that nothing sexual is indicated in these words. That is correct. But that observation exposes a very skewed view of homosexuality among critics. Homosexuality is not just about physical, sexual activity. It is as multifaceted in its care and expression as heterosexuality.

In another case, when David expresses grief

over the death of his friend Jonathan, he says, "My brother Jonathan; greatly beloved were you to me; your love to me was wonderful, passing the love of women" (2 Sam 1:26). These words may simply be poetic or even political. But they might also be more. How we read them is often dependent upon our cultural lens and personal sensitivities.

Just for Fun

A great irony. The words spoken to Naomi by Ruth have been used at innumerable weddings as a beautiful, verbal description of the marriage covenant and relationship. But when applied to Ruth and Naomi as covenantal language (in the original context in which they were spoken!), some people recoil.

***

9. Being LGBTQ Is a Choice

The Challenge
LGBTQ identities are a choice and therefore a sin. The Bible doesn't teach that God created gay or transgendered people.

The Response
I am exactly who God created me to be, and God always looks at God's creation and says, "It is good."

The Explanation
In the creation story of Genesis 1, we catch a glimpse of the essence of a mysterious, invisible God. The writer gives a summation of the sixth day of creation by saying, "God created humankind in his image, in the image of God he created them; male and female he created them." In humanity we get a glimpse of God.

No one individual can hold the essence of God's image, and no single gender can hold the essence of God's image. For humanity to reflect the image of God, both male and female had to be created. The truth behind such a disclosure is simple: God cannot be reduced to one gender. God, in God's self, is both. If God holds both, does it not stand to reason that while we are typically gender-identified, we are all capable of holding some mixture of both? Science bears this out. Our own observations bear this out. The very first story of biblical text suggests we have the capacity to be a mysterious mix of gender and sexual orientation.

More specific are the words of Jesus. In Matthew 19 the disciples are quizzically responding to a discussion between Jesus and some religious leaders regarding marriage and divorce. Jesus ends the conversation with a strange and interesting statement: "Not everyone can accept this teaching, but only those to whom it is given. For there are eunuchs who have been so from birth, and there are eunuchs who have been made eunuchs by others, and there are eunuchs who have made themselves eunuchs for the sake of the kingdom of heaven. Let anyone accept this who can."

Jesus is clear in his prefacing and concluding remarks: this is a truth that will be hard for many to accept. What part of this is hard? It was not an anomaly during the biblical era for a person to submit to castration in order to serve in the palace of royalty. It was not strange for a young boy to be sold into slavery and castrated for service in the palace of royalty. (Eunuchs posed no threat to the kings' wives and concubines.) The hard part of this text is the following: "There are eunuchs who have been so from birth." Jesus is not speaking of children born without genitalia, a rarity that is hardly worth mentioning. It makes more sense to identify these persons as homosexual or transgender. These would be persons who appeared, acted, and were comfortable being more effeminate or were known to be committed to a same-sex partner and thus posed no threat to the king's harem. Jesus sees value in each of these persons, not just relative to an earthly kingdom, but to the kingdom of heaven. Jesus in no way judges these individuals, but rather seems to elevate their gift amid the messy world of marriage.

Both Old and New Testaments affirm the wonderful array of God's creation with regard to sexual orientation and gender.

Just for Fun

Here is an excerpt from a sermon I preached during the summer of 2014. The biblical text was Acts 8:26–39. I promise it's not long.

The Ethiopian eunuch *chose* to be a eunuch, and he was *born* a foreigner— an Ethiopian. Allow me to say it again. He *chose* to be a eunuch and was *born* a foreigner. According to Deuteronomy 23 he was disqualified from being part of the family of faith on both counts. No one whose testicles were crushed could be part of the family of faith, and no foreigner could be part of the family of faith. This was the Jewish faith of the Old Testament. But when his chariot came upon a body of water, the eunuch asked Philip, "Is there anything that hinders me from being baptized?" And Philip went down into the water with him and baptized him.

Now here's the deal. When he came out of the water, he was still an Ethiopian—the way he was born. When he came out of the water, he was still a eunuch—the result of his choice. We love to discuss whether people choose to be the way they are or are born the way they are—as if God really cares, as if it really matters, as if we can divide the miraculous mix of our nature and our choices. The Ethiopian eunuch lived with both realities in his life—continued to live with both realities in his life—and even though there was a verse in Deuteronomy that seemed to condemn him, God accepted him.

***

PART 2

Welcoming & Affirming
Churches and the Bible

1. You Are Not a True Baptist

The Challenge

You are not a true Baptist if you allow for the baptism, marriage, ordination, and other faith service and faith expressions of LGBTQ persons.

The Response

True Baptists claim the freedom to worship and serve God as they deem fit under the leadership of the Holy Spirit. And they afford others the freedom to do the same.

The Explanation

(I am a minister in the Baptist faith expression. I know many readers may not be a part of or familiar with this faith expression. I begin here, however, because it is at the center of my daily experience. It is here where I am challenged most. If you have no interest in the Baptist expression, feel free to skip this challenge, response, and explanation and read on.)

Among the distinguishing characteristics of being Baptist are soul freedom and the autonomy of the local church. Soul freedom preserves the right of every Christian to read the Bible and interpret it as they are led under the direction of God's Spirit. Baptists have historically rejected any creedal statements by which the church or any other entity imposes any belief on the individual. The mystery of God and the mystery of God's ways cannot be held or monopolized by any one interpretation.

The autonomy of the local church takes this faith freedom a step further. Each church—each congregation—has the right to decide how it will practice faith under the leadership of God's Spirit. One Baptist church does not dictate the practices of any other Baptist church. We may decide to cooperate with each other in common mission endeavors (thus, the establishment of the Southern Baptist Convention or the Cooperative Baptist Fellowship), but we do not claim the status of a denomination that is defined by a system of hierarchy and top-down governance. Each church is autonomous and chooses to convene with other churches to accomplish God's work in the world.

While I may be critical of more conservative approaches to biblical interpretation and church polity, I would never accuse another Baptist or Baptist church of 'not being Baptist' because they do not believe or practice faith like me. They have every right to live faith—both individually and corporately—as they choose. So, for any Baptist to say, "You are not a true Baptist if _____," is an indication that *they* do not understand what it means to be Baptist.

Just for Fun
While attending a convention of Southern Baptists a couple decades ago, a participant at the convention proposed a resolution that would prohibit churches from hiring women as pastors. The person sitting next to me was new to Baptist faith and polity. He leaned over and asked, "Can they enforce a policy like that on churches?"

"Not really," I said. "Resolutions are not binding on local churches. But they may choose to kick you out of the convention if you deviate from them."

He continued, "So do you believe a church should have the right to call a female minister?"

"If a local congregation wants to call a female, green, lesbian kangaroo just released from prison to be its pastor, it has every right to do so. No one can tell the local congregation how to live its faith. That's what it means to be Baptist—for better or for worse."

***

2. You Do Not Take Moral Teachings Seriously

The Challenge
If you welcome and affirm the LGBTQ community, you are not taking the moral teachings of the Bible seriously.

The Response
While we truly rest in the grace of God, we also take seriously the intent and moral teachings of the Bible as we understand them.

The Explanation
It is important to truly study the Bible. It is important (particularly when attacking or critiquing the life of another) that we dig beneath the surface of Scripture, beneath the English translation of obscure words, and beneath the biases of our own culture to find the true intent of the text. It is also important that we avoid fear-based arguments and propaganda. How many times have I heard someone argue, "If you accept homosexuals, it's just a slippery slope? The next thing you'll do is embrace pedophilia and bestiality."

This is a fear-based argument that holds no real truth. In fact, the Bible is very clear with regard to pedophilia, bestiality, and any other forms of sex without consent—it is not condoned. The gospel is clearly and morally opposed to treating people like property or treating people as less than human. These are the clear morals of Jesus; ironically, these are also the moral demands ignored by those who reject the LGBTQ community.

Just for Fun

A former church member invited me to coffee to share with me why they were leaving the church.

"Jim, I love the church, and I love people, but if we allow gay people to participate in the rituals of the church, we aren't taking our morals seriously. I can't be part of any institution that looks the other way or, worse, accepts what I think is a sinful lifestyle."

"I get it," I said. "Thanks for sharing this with me face-to-face rather than just quietly slipping away."

"Well, we're friends, and I wanted you to know how I feel."

"So," I asked, "what are you doing this weekend?"

"College football, baby! It should be a great game."

"Well, I'm just guessing, but I imagine there are some players on the team who are gay. And I would be willing to bet there are gay students, professors, and administrators at the university. And I'm pretty sure, given a crowd that large, there will be gay persons in the stands. I'm a little shocked that you would go and actually 'cheer' for that team, proudly wear that team's colors, desire the best for that team's future, and—to use your words—be part of an institution that doesn't take their morals seriously."

"That's not church; that's just football."

"Just football?" I sarcastically responded. "You spend one hour in church on Sunday. I'd again be willing to bet you spend more time, money, conversation, and thought on college football than you do on church. That's not intended as a judgment; that's just truth. And isn't it strange that you insist on moral living in the church but not in a part of the world that garners your enthusiastic investment and support?"

"Well, I hear you," he thoughtfully responded, "but I don't expect football players to be perfect."

"And I don't expect church members to be perfect. I just want us all to be welcome in the presence of God so that God can do God's good work in us—all of us."

***

3. You Are Going to Hell for Being Welcoming

The Challenge
You're going to hell for welcoming and affirming the LGBTQ community.

The Response
Our relationship with God and our future in the presence of God is completely dependent upon our profession of faith in God through the grace of Jesus Christ. If anything, the love and mercy we extend to others—including the LGBTQ community—is an indication of the authenticity of our faith in God.

The Explanation
First John is a short New Testament epistle, but it packs a powerful punch. It is John who makes the short but wonderful statement "God is love." It is John who asserts that we best show our love toward God by loving one another. He even goes on to say that if we do not love one another, we cannot claim to love God.

Theologically, our eternal destiny will not be sacrificed by showing love to the LGBTQ community. God is not looking down from God's heaven and nullifying our baptisms when we are nice to homosexuals. In fact, if John is correct (and most of our critics believe the Bible), the opposite may be true. The merciless rejection of LGBTQ persons may impede access to our heavenly abode.

Since God is love, I would rather stand before God one day and be told, "You loved too much. You shared love with too many people. You were too liberal in your love and mercy and grace," rather than, "You did not love enough. You did not love the people I loved. You withheld love from those who needed it most."

The Bible states over and over again that the merciful will receive mercy. We will be judged in the manner we judge. We will be forgiven as we forgive. Again, if the Bible is true (and I believe it is), I do not think those who mercifully, lovingly, gracefully love and welcome the LGBTQ community are the ones in danger of God's judgment.

Just for Fun

Our church was recently picketed and protested for welcoming and including the LGBTQ community. One of the protestors carried a poster that read, "GOD'S LOVE WON'T KEEP YOU OUT OF HELL." I am still pondering the theological ignorance of that statement. I thought God's love *was* the only thing that delivers us from hell.

***

4. You Are a False Teacher

The Challenge

You are a false teacher if you advocate for the welcome and inclusion of the LGBTQ community.

The Response

What we teach about love, grace, mercy, and acceptance of the LGBTQ community is absolutely consistent with the life and teachings of Jesus and the early church.

The Explanation

The old covenant between God and Israel (expressed in the writings of the Old Testament) was primarily a *conditional* covenant. In other words, *if* Israel was obedient, *then* God would embrace them as God's children. This covenant inherently is a covenant of exclusion. Only those who manage to keep the law are in. All who do not keep the law are out.

The new covenant (expressed in the life and teachings of Jesus, as well as the writings of the early church recorded in the New Testament) is an *unconditional* covenant. *Because* we cannot keep the law perfectly, and *because* we realize no particular group of people have a monopoly on God, and *because* Jesus was representative of God's love for all humanity, the new covenant is inherently inclusive.

False teaching in the New Testament is typically an accusation made toward persons who question the divine work of Jesus in the world. It does not refer to differences of interpretation or opinion regarding the practice of faith in Jesus. Even the apostle Paul admits differences among the churches with regard to faith practice and faith expression. The early church also transparently struggles with this issue in Acts 15 regarding the Old Testament mandate of circumcision. In this story we watch the council of Christians in Jerusalem argue a matter of Old Testament law, set the mandate of the law aside, and settle on the side of grace and inclusion. The law said persons of faith had to be circumcised. The church decided— under the leadership of the Holy Spirit—people did not have to be circumcised to have faith.

When we teach the unconditional love, grace, and inclusive work of the gospel, this is not sharing false information. I'm more suspicious of a proposed gospel that is conditional.

Just for Fun

I accidentally answered the telephone—again. As soon as I said "Jim Dant," the caller burst into a sermonic cacophony I thought would never end. It was a harsh and harrowing mix of scriptures and exhortations and accusations, interrupted by deep draws of breath providing fuel for the next extended bellow. Finally, the caller reached a crescendo and literally screamed into the telephone, "You are a false teacher! You are the whore of Babylon who comes to deceive the world."

And then silence. The only sound was his breathing…breathing…breathing like a dog on the hunt waiting for its prey to make a move.

I finally mustered my thoughts and responded.

"Well," I said, "since we are talking about issues of sexuality and gender and since you are obviously appalled at anything having a whiff of

homosexuality or transgender, you should proba-
bly refer to me as the gigolo of Babylon rather than
the whore of Babylon."

He hung up.

***

5. You Are Not Biblical

The Challenge
You are not biblical if you teach the welcome and inclusion of LGBTQ persons into the faith.

The Response
A close reading of both Old and New Testaments reveals an ongoing broadening of the faith. God's people are consistently moving toward expansive grace and broad inclusion.

The Explanation
In the Old Testament it is made clear in Deuteronomy 23:3 that no Moabite may be admitted into the assembly of the Lord. None of their descendants may be admitted to the assembly of the Lord. That is a verse in the Bible; that is the law. In Isaiah 56, however, the prophet argues on behalf of foreigners who wish to keep the Lord's Sabbath and covenant. They may be admitted to the assembly of the Lord. He goes on to pen these famous words: "My (God's) house shall be a house of prayer for all people."

By the time we get to the book of Ruth, Ruth 4 shares the story of a Jewish landowner, Boaz, marrying a Moabite woman named Ruth. Both Boaz and the Jewish community welcome her into the faith family of God. As for her descendants (remember, no Moabite or their descendants were to receive a place in the assembly of the Lord), she becomes the great-grandmother of King David and a part of the ancestral family of Jesus. Even the conditional covenant of the Old Testament evolved to be more graceful and inclusive than the letter of the law.

This evolution of grace is even more vivid in the New Testament book of Acts. The first followers of Jesus were almost exclusively Jewish, and the named disciples were almost exclusively male. Peter, one of the disciples, stands to preach in Acts 2 during the Festival of Pentecost and proclaims God's Spirit is going to fall on Jews and Greeks, men and women, slaves and free persons. This was unheard of! The subsequent stories, recorded in the book of Acts, are a record of this expanding work of the Spirit and grace. Women are the nucleus of new churches. Roman prison guards and soldiers become numbered among the believers. An Ethiopian eunuch is welcomed into the waters of baptism. Gentiles are relieved of circumcision laws and are fused into the faith family. All of these persons—every last one of them—could have been excluded from the church based on a verse in the Bible. The Bible, however, inherently allows for the maturing and evolution of faith.

Before Jesus' death and resurrection he met with his disciples and shared these words with them: "I will give you the keys of the kingdom of heaven, and whatever you bind on earth will be bound in heaven, and whatever you loose on earth will be loosed in heaven." Jesus, in essence, gave us the responsibility of shaping the Christian community. We decide who is in and who is out. We prayerfully determine what is permitted and what is prohibited. In essence, Jesus is saying that heaven will bless our efforts. Given such a great responsibility and power, it seems the church would always lean toward love, grace, mercy, and inclusion. This is the obvious progression of both

Old and New Testaments. This is the obvious intent of the heart of God and God's revelation of self in Jesus Christ. This is the nature of judgment I wish to face in heaven—one of love, grace, mercy, and inclusion. I must judge in the same manner I wish to be judged and received.

There is nothing more biblical than the practice of love, grace, and inclusion. Excluding a person on the basis of a verse goes against the ongoing stories of God, Jesus, and the church as they are revealed in the Bible. Quoting a verse and excluding a soul does not honor the Bible or God.

***

EPILOGUE

You owe no assailant a thorough explanation of your beliefs. Most of your critics could not provide a cohesive theological explanation of their beliefs beyond, "There's a verse in the Bible that says…" Second, they are not in conversation with you to be convinced of anything themselves. It is not a true dialogue. They are not thinking. They are simply protecting their ideas, dogma, and personal fears from the intrusion of grace. Sadly, people who fail to offer grace have rarely allowed themselves to enjoy the full measure of grace afforded them. In the end they are trying to condemn or convince you. So use these arguments if you wish, or simply hold them close and sing with confidence, "Jesus loves me; this I know. For the Bible tells me so."

INVITE JIM

If your church or organization is interested in delving deeper into the ideas contained in *This I Know: A Simple Biblical Defense for LGBTQ Christians*, schedule a retreat, conference, or other event with Jim Dant. Jim is a frequent retreat, conference, and guest speaker with regard to the material in this book, as well as many other topics.

Other titles available by Jim Dant:

1 & 2 Samuel: Surviving the Tensions of Life

The Truth Is Sensational Enough

Pray the Trail: A Contemplative Walk on the Ocmulgee Heritage Trail

How Does the Church Decide?

One Pastor, Twelve Steps: My Journey through the Valley of the Shadow of Addiction

Finding Your Voice: How to Speak Your Heart's True Faith

For booking information, please contact Jim directly at jim@faithlab.com.

CPSIA information can be obtained
at www.ICGtesting.com
Printed in the USA
LVHW081653050323
740989LV00017B/1669